This Coloring Book belongs to:

_____

Coloring Book

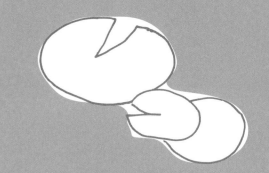

Claude Monet

PRESTEL

Munich · London · New York

That's Claude Monet, the painter.

He lived about a hundred years ago near Paris, in France.

Claude Monet used to paint impressions of the things he saw. He recorded on canvas what things looked like at that moment. The moment when the sun rises and everything looks a delicate pink. The warm yellow light of sunset. The blue mist hanging over the River Seine. The sunbeam that tickles your nose...

An entire art movement was named after his style of painting: the artists were called Impressionists.

Almost as famous as Monet's paintings were his house and garden in Giverny, the village where he and his large family lived. Monet's favorite spot was by his pond, where he liked to sit and paint his Japanese bridge and the water lilies.

Claude Monet painting by the water lily pond.

In this book, you will find pictures by Claude Monet to paint and finish. Use the colors you like the most, and paint the pictures the way you like.

In this photo, Claude Monet is about 24 years old.

Here is a picture of Camille, Claude's wife.
What color is her dress?

That's Jean, Claude and Camille's son. Can you finish the pictures?

Seed pod

Poppy

Blossom

Bud

Poppies were Claude's favorite flowers.

Who will you paint in the poppy field?

Hollyhock

Rose

Sunflower

Day lilies

Clematis

Bearded irises

All these flowers still grow in Monet's garden.

Claude's friends have picked bunches of flowers in his garden.

Would you like to paint a colorful flowerbed?

The water lily pond!

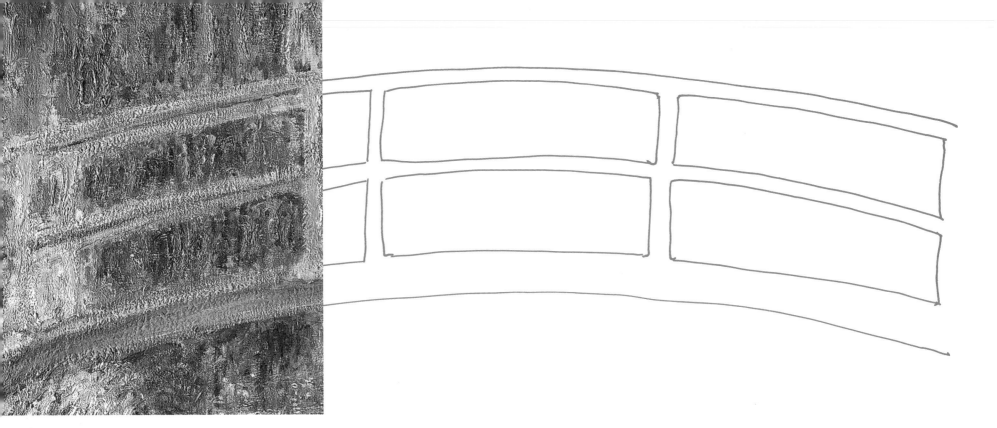

A Japanese bridge crosses Claude's pond.

Here, Camille is dressed up in a
Japanese dress.

In summer, Claude's children liked to go fishing in the boat.

Picnic time...

A fishing boat out at sea.

The sun is rising!

Where's the train going?

Claude Monet's Original Pictures.

Here you can see the pictures by Claude Monet that were used in this book. Do you recognize any of them?

1 *Camille* or *The Woman in a Green Dress*, 1866. Kunsthalle, Bremen.
Photograph: Artothek
2 *Field of Poppies near Argenteuil*, 1873. Musée d'Orsay, Paris. Photograph: Artothek
3 *Luncheon*, 1873. Musée d'Orsay, Paris. Photograph: Artothek
4 *Water Lilies, Evening*, 1899. Musée Marmottan, Paris. Photograph: Bridgeman
5 *Jean Monet on His Hobby Horse*, 1872. The Metropolitan Museum of Art, New York. Gift of Sara Lee Corporation, 2000. Photograph: Artothek

6 *Still Life with Sunflowers*, 1880. The Metropolitan Museum of Art, New York. Photograph: Artothek
7 *Women in the Garden*, 1866–67. Musée d'Orsay, Paris. Photograph: Artothek
8 *The Water Lily Pond*, 1899. The Trustees of the National Gallery, London. Photograph: Artothek
9 *The Gare Saint-Lazare: Arrival of a Train*, 1877. Fogg Art Museum, Harvard University Art Museums, Cambridge, Massachusetts. Bequest from the Collection of Maurice Wertheim, Class of 1906

10 *Impression—Sunrise*, 1873. Musée Marmottan, Paris. Photograph: Artothek
11 *Camille in Japanese Costume*, 1875. Museum of Fine Arts, Boston
12 *In the Boat*, 1887. Musée d'Orsay, Paris
13 *Seascape During a Storm*, 1867. Sterling and Francine Clark Art Institute, Williamstown, Massachusetts
14 *Luncheon on the Grass* (Central Panel), 1865–66. Musée d'Orsay, Paris. Photograph: Artothek

© Prestel Verlag
Munich · London · New York 2006. 9th printing 2015

Prestel, a member of
Verlagsgruppe Random House GmbH

Prestel Verlag
www.prestel.de

Prestel Publishing Ltd.
14-17 Wells Street
London W1T 3PD

Prestel Publishing
900 Broadway, Suite 603
New York, N.Y. 10003
www.prestel.com

Library of Congress Control Number is available.

British Library Cataloguing-in-Publication Data
A catalogue record for this book is available from the British Library.

The Deutsche Bibliothek holds a record of this publication in the Deutsche Nationalbibliografie; detailed bibliographical data can be found under: http://dnb.ddb.de

Prestel books are available worldwide. Please contact your nearest bookseller or one of the above addresses for information concerning your local distributor.

Concept and drawings by Doris Kutschbach
Translated from the German by Paul Aston
Design and Production by Claudia Weyh, Carolina Fahrentholz
Origination by Reproline Genceller, Munich
Printing and binding: Lanarepro GmbH, Lana

FSC
www.fsc.org
MIX
From responsible sources
FSC® C016410

Verlagsgruppe Random House FSC® N001967
The FSC®-certified paper Tauro has been supplied by Papier Union GmbH, Gemany.

ISBN 978-3-7913-3713-5

Bearded iris